Those Delightful Dolphins

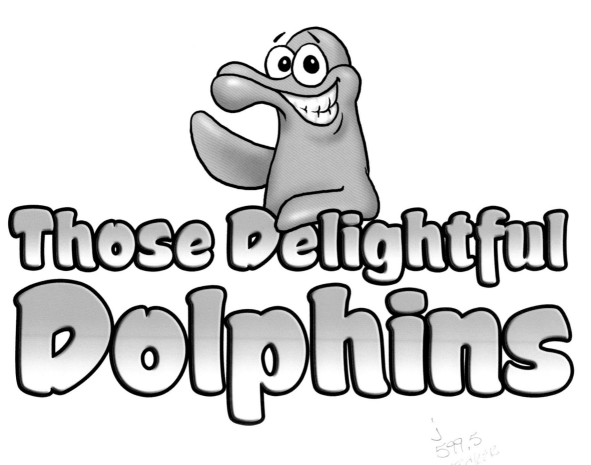

Those Delightful Dolphins

Jan Lee Wicker

Illustrated by Steve Weaver

Pineapple Press, Inc.
Sarasota, Florida

Photos on pages 14, 22, 26, 30, 32, 36, 38 courtesy of Marineland's Dolphin Conservation Center.
Photos on pages 8, 20 (bottom), 24, 42 courtesy of the Wild Dolphin Project.
Photo on page 2 by Marc M. Ellis, H2OPICTURES. Website: www.h2opictures.com.
Photo on page 18 courtesy of Mote Marine Laboratory.
Photos on pages 12, 16, 28 by Chris Wicker.
Photos on pages 20 (top), 40 by Jan Lee Wicker

Inquiries should be addressed to:
Pineapple Press, Inc.
P.O. Box 3889
Sarasota, Florida 34230

www.pineapplepress.com

Library of Congress Cataloging-in-Publication Data
Wicker, Jan Lee, 1953-
Those delightful dolphins / Jan Lee Wicker. -- 1st ed.
p. cm.
Includes index.
ISBN 978-1-56164-380-6 (hardback : alk. paper) --
ISBN 978-1-56164-381-3 (pbk. : alk. paper)
1. Dolphins--Juvenile literature. I. Title.
QL737.C432W53 2007
599.53--dc22
2007000066

First Edition
Hb 10 9 8 7 6 5 4 3 2 1
Pb 10 9 8 7 6 5 4 3 2 1

Design by Steve Weaver

Printed in China

To Paul and Meagan, who surf with the dolphins

Many thanks to Bill Hurley of Marineland for his invaluable help on this book.
A special thanks also to Cindy Rogers of the Wild Dolphin Project.

Contents

spotted dolphin
and calf

mahi-mahi

Is a dolphin a fish?

No. A dolphin is a small whale. Like whales, it is a mammal. It doesn't have gills like a fish. It has to come up for air to breathe. Dolphins are warm-blooded just like we are. A dolphin has live babies. They even have a belly button. Dolphins nurse their young. A calf (baby dolphin) has whiskers on its rostrum (nose or beak). These help the baby find its mother. (But just to confuse things, there is a fish that some people call a dolphin. Another name for it is mahi-mahi. Let's all call it that so we won't get it confused with the mammal this book is about!)

9

dorsal fin

nostrum

melon

flukes

blowhole

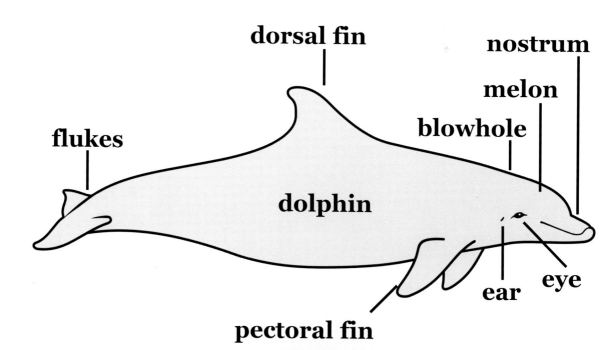

dolphin

ear

eye

pectoral fin

second
dorsal fin

dorsal fin

eye

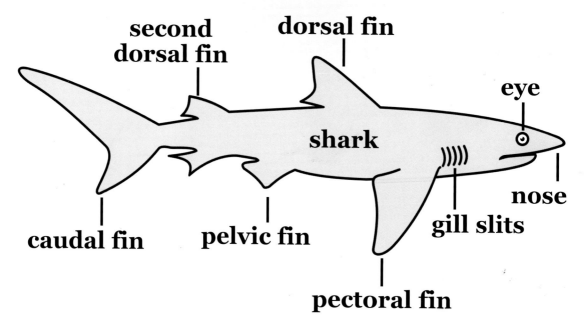

shark

caudal fin

pelvic fin

gill slits

nose

pectoral fin

How can you tell the difference between a dolphin and a shark?

A dolphin's dorsal fin (the one on its back) is more curved than a shark's. A dolphin's flukes (tail) are horizontal (flat) and move up and down as it swims. A shark's tail is vertical like its dorsal fin and it moves from side to side as it swims.

How do dolphins breathe?

A dolphin breathes through a blowhole. This can be found on the top of the head between the dorsal fin and the rostrum. The blowhole is not for smelling like a nose is. The water that seems to be coming out of a dolphin's blowhole is from air being pushed out. This is called spouting. It closes its blowhole just like you would hold your nose to go underwater. A dolphin can hold its breath for 7–10 minutes. Most people can hold their breath for less than a minute.

How do dolphins communicate?

They squeak, click, whistle, and grunt. Dolphins can click 2,000 times per second. Each female has a unique (one of a kind) whistle. Male dolphins have a whistle similar to their mother's. Just like people, dolphins also use body language to communicate. They clap their jaws, nod their heads, slap their flippers, and twist their bodies. When dolphins clap their jaws they are ready to fight. This is the same as people clenching their fists.

How well can dolphins hear?

Dolphins can hear very well. They don't have outer earlobes. They have ear holes behind their eyes. Dolphins use echolocation just like bats. Their high-pitched sounds bounce off objects and echo back. This way the dolphin can tell the position, distance, and size of a shark or other fish.

melon

How do dolphins make their sounds?

On the top of a dolphin's head is a fatty area known as a melon. A dolphin's sounds are made with the melon. Part of the melon is called the "monkey lips." This helps make the sounds. If you blow up a balloon then squeeze the neck of the balloon you will hear high squeaky sounds. The whistles dolphins make come through the monkey lips. The monkey lips act like the neck of a balloon to make the noises.

This dolphin has been injured by a shark.

What are a dolphin's enemies?

Sharks, orcas (killer whales), and humans. Dolphin bones have been found in tiger and bull sharks. Dolphins have killed sharks (in defense) by ramming them with their rostrums. Many dolphins have been killed by humans for meat, leather, and oil. Pollution, boat traffic, and destroying dolphin habitats (where dolphins live) have been big reasons for dolphin deaths.

Do dolphins have teeth?

Yes. Bottlenose dolphins have 40–52 teeth in their upper jaws. They have 36–48 teeth in their lower jaws. Humans only have 32 teeth. A dolphin's teeth are for grasping, not for chewing. They swallow their food whole. Scientists can tell the age of a dolphin by looking at their teeth. They count the growth rings on the inside of dolphin's teeth. There is one  ring for every year the dolphin has lived. Bottlenose dolphins live to be about 25 years old.

This spotted dolphin is
searching for food on the
ocean bottom.

What do dolphins eat?

The bottlenose dolphin's favorite foods are fish and squid. They also eat shrimp, crabs, eels, and stingrays. Most dolphins eat about 30 pounds of food a day. Larger dolphins like the orcas eat whales, other dolphins, seals, birds, sea otters, and sea turtles. They eat 400 pounds of food each day. Dolphins don't drink the salty water they live in. They get water from the food they eat.

Can dolphins see well?

Yes. They can see well both in the water and above the water. One thing that helps them do this is the jellylike liquid that their eyes make. This helps protect their eyes from the salt water. Scientists have discovered that dolphins can see in color. Dolphins recognize blues and greens.

How fast can dolphins swim?

Some dolphins swim as fast as 24 miles per hour for short distances. That's the same speed you ride in a car around town. Dolphins have been known to dive as deep as 3,280 feet. That is like a dolphin diving down past 2 ½ Empire State buildings.

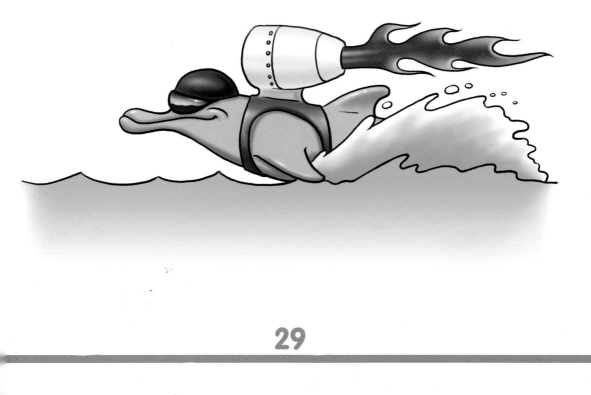

How high can dolphins jump out of the water?

They have been seen jumping 16 feet above the water. When dolphins leap out of water and fall back in the water sideways it is called breaching. One way for dolphins to move through the water is by porpoising. It happens when dolphins are going through the water and they come up to breathe. They come out of the water and go back in headfirst. When dolphins are in a hurry, they will porpoise through the water very fast.

How big is a dolphin?

Bottlenose dolphins can grow to be 8–12 feet. The ceiling in your classroom is probably about 8 feet tall. Dolphins weigh a lot because they have blubber (body fat) to keep them warm. Bottlenose dolphins weigh 400–500 pounds. The smallest dolphin is the Commerson's dolphin. It is only 5 feet long. It weighs around 130 pounds. The largest dolphin is the orca. It is 33 feet long and weighs 3–9 tons. That is as much as a car or truck weighs.

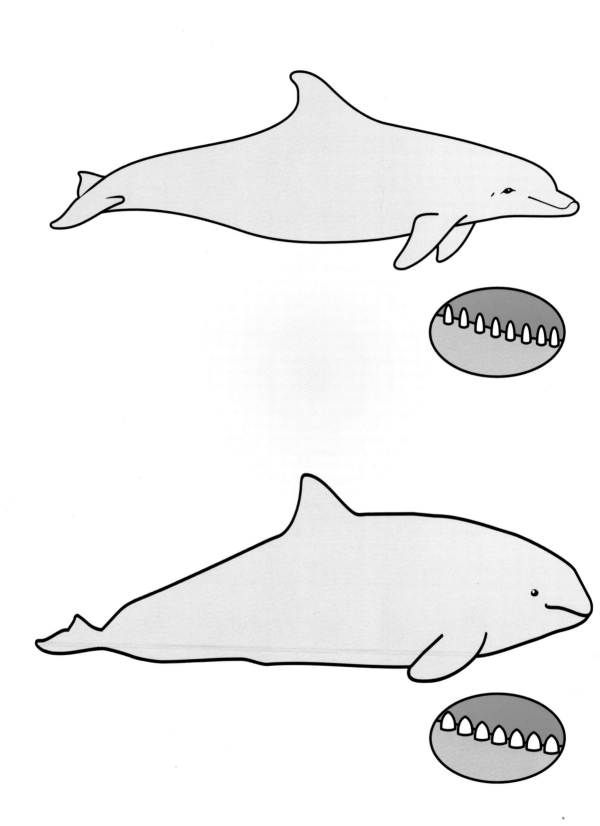

What is the difference between a dolphin and a porpoise?

Both are mammals and look a lot alike, but there are some differences between them. The body of the porpoise is fatter. The head of a porpoise is rounder. Most dolphins have a pointed beak, but most porpoises' beaks are more round. The dolphin's fin is more wave-shaped. Porpoises have triangle-shaped fins. The teeth of a porpoise are like flat shovels. The dolphin's teeth are like sharp cones. Dolphins are easier to spot since porpoises are shy.

This pregnant dolphin is having an ultrasound to check her baby.

This dolphin is having blood drawn.

Why do people train dolphins?

Dolphins can be taught certain behaviors for their medical care. They are taught to lay their flukes in their trainer's lap so blood samples can be taken. Trainers teach dolphins to beach themselves on a pool deck scale to be weighed. Dolphins will allow tubes to be put down their throats and into their stomachs. Then they can be given extra water or medicine. Brushing a dolphin's teeth is no problem when the dolphin is rewarded for opening its mouth. Dolphins are trained by hand signals to do these behaviors for the dolphin's and trainer's safety. Some of these behaviors can be seen in shows for people's enjoyment.

How smart are dolphins and what can they do?

Most dolphins are wild and behave as they need to in order to survive. Many animals, like dolphins, can be trained by people to do a natural behavior on command. This is done by rewarding them with food. Dolphins like other rewards in addition to food. Some enjoy playing with balls or hoops. Others like a scratch or belly rub. A dolphin likes to twirl in the water. When you teach it to hold a paintbrush, it can paint a picture by twirling.

How can you tell dolphins apart?

Scientists use the dorsal fin to tell dolphins apart. This fin is 1–1½ feet high. A dolphin's fin can get cuts and notches in it from the dolphin's actions. Just like our fingerprints, each fin is different. By looking at the fins, scientists track the dolphins to learn information about them. They can compare changes in a dolphin's health and learn about dolphin behavior.

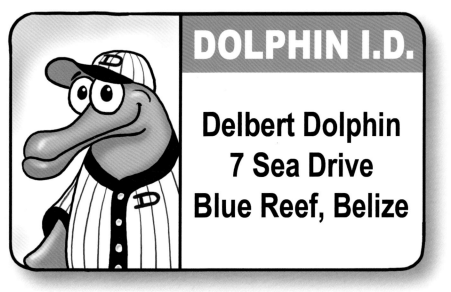

DOLPHIN I.D.

**Delbert Dolphin
7 Sea Drive
Blue Reef, Belize**

How many babies do dolphins have?

Dolphins have one baby at a time every 2–3 years. The mother is pregnant for almost a year before its calf is born. A newborn calf is 3 feet long and weighs 36 pounds. A calf is darker than an adult. The calf nurses 6 months to 1½ years. When nursing it curls its tongue up just like people can do. Then it sticks its tongue inside one of the 2 holes on the mother's belly. Using muscles, the mother pumps milk through the calf's tongue. The baby can eat fish at 6 months old. Dolphins stay with their mothers until they are 2–3 years old.

Bottlenose

Striped

Hourglass

Spinner

Spotted

How many different kinds of saltwater dolphins are there?

There are 33 kinds of saltwater dolphins. They are found everywhere in the world except near the North Pole and in Antarctica. The bottlenose dolphin is the most often seen. Many are seen off the coast of North Carolina and Florida. The striped dolphin has a thin, dark stripe along its side. The hourglass dolphin is black and white with a black eye patch and stripe. The adult spotted dolphin has spots. A spinner dolphin spins in the air when it leaps out of the water.

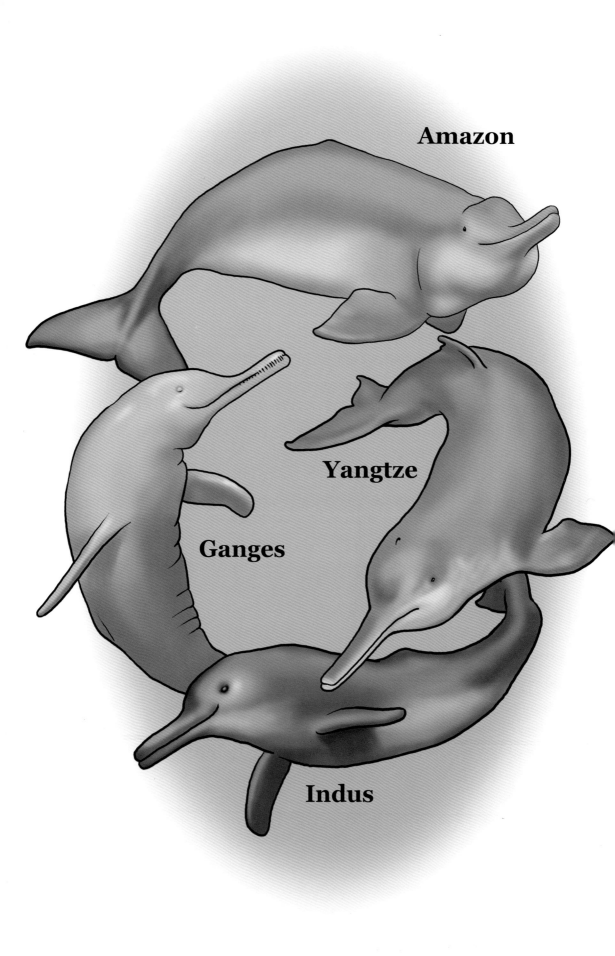

Amazon

Yangtze

Ganges

Indus

Are dolphins endangered?

Yes, many of the freshwater dolphins are endangered, and one may be extinct. The Amazon River dolphin is the largest freshwater dolphin. There are many of these left. The other three freshwater dolphins are endangered. The Ganges River dolphin is almost blind. The Indus and Yangtze dolphins, which are found in Asia, are also endangered. At one time many dolphins were getting caught in fishing nets. When dolphins were caught in tuna nets they couldn't breathe and would drown. Now tuna fishermen use  safer nets to help dolphins. If you eat canned tuna, look for the label that shows it is dolphin-safe.

Dolphinarium

You will need:

cream cheese

blue food coloring

gummy dolphins

favorite cracker

plastic knife

Add a few drops of blue food coloring to the cream cheese and mix it up to make the cream cheese blue. Use the knife to spread the cream cheese onto the cracker. Add a few gummy dolphins to make your dolphinarium. Make as many as you can eat!

Colorful Dolphin

You will need:

dolphin pattern *

2 sponges

pencil

2 colors of tempera paint

white paper

water

paper towels

scissors

pan for paint (an old pie pan or cleaned-out meat tray)

* Use the one shown at left. Enlarge it on a photocopy machine.

Wet a sponge and squeeze out the water. Use a paper towel to squeeze it out some more. Put a little paint (start with the darker color first) into a pan. Dab the sponge into the paint. (Remember that with sponge paint you want to see the texture of the sponge so don't get the sponge too wet.) Lightly dab the paint-covered sponge around the white paper. Do the same thing with the second color, just lightly around the paper. Let the paper dry overnight. Use a pencil to trace the dolphin pattern onto the back of the paper. Cut it out and show your friends!

Handprint dolphin

You will need:

blue tempera paint   white paper

Dip the side of your hand in the paint. Cup your hand slightly and print it on the paper. This makes the body and part of the tail. Use your pinky to add the other fluke of the tail. Add more paint to your pinky and make the rostrum and 2 flippers. For the dorsal fin, use your pinky again—stick it straight up and curl it down to make the dorsal fin curved. Practice until you get it right.

Diving Dolphin

You will need:

large flat pan   blue liquid tempera paint
clear dish washing liquid   a few tablespoons of water
dolphin pattern*   straw
water   white paper
1 sheet of colored foam paper   scissors
pencil   glue

*Use the one shown at left. Enlarge it on a photocopy machine.

In the pan add about half blue paint and half dishwashing liquid with a few tablespoons of water until the bottom of the pan is covered. (You may have to experiment with the amounts until you get the bubbles blowing.) Point the straw straight into the liquid and start to blow bubbles. When you have blown a lot of bubbles, take your paper and quickly press the paper on top of the bubbles, popping them as you go—don't let your paper touch the liquid, just the bubbles. Make several papers and let them dry overnight. Trace your pattern on top of the foam and cut out your dolphin. Glue it on top of your bubble paper.

Glossary

blowhole – the opening a dolphin uses to breathe, which is found on the top of the head

breaching – leaping out of the water and falling back in the water sideways

calf – baby dolphin

dorsal fin – the fin on the back of a dolphin or a shark, which can be seen sticking out of the water

echolocation (ek-o-loh-*kay*-shun) – how objects are found by how long it takes for sound to echo back

endangered – animals that are few in number and in danger of becoming extinct, usually due to their changing environment

extinct – an animal that has died out completely

fluke – each side of a dolphin's tail

horizontal – level or flat; the top of a table is horizontal

melon – fatty area on a dolphin's head

orca – the largest dolphin and the fastest swimming sea mammal; also known as a killer whale

porpoising – when a dolphin comes out of the water to breathe while swimming

rostrum – nose or beak of a dolphin

spouting – when water is blown straight up from the air being forced out of the blowhole

vertical – straight up and down; walls in a house are vertical

Where to Learn More about Dolphins

Books

Crisp, Marty. *Everything Dolphin*. Minnetonka, MN: Northwood Press, 2004.

Dudzinski, Kathleen. *Meeting Dolphins: My Adventures in the Sea*. Washington, DC: National Geographic Society, 2000.

Kingfisher, Christianne Gunzi. *The Best Book of Whales and Dolphins*. Boston, MA: Houghton-Mifflin, 2001.

Maden, Mary. *The Dolphin Adventure*. Kill Devil Hills, NC: Dog and Pony Publishing, 2002.

Spilsbury, Richard and Louise. *A School of Dolphins*. Chicago, IL: Heinemann Library, 2004.

Vogel, Julia. *Our Wild World Series: Dolphins*. Minnetonka, MN: Northwood Press, 2001.

Some Good Dolphin Websites

www.marineland.net
Enjoy dolphins up close!

www.wilddolphinproject.org
Lots of dolphin games.

www.capelookoutstudies.org
Try the fin-matching game.

www.nationalgeographic.com/kids
Watch a video of dolphins and more.

About the Author

Jan Lee Wicker has taught children in pre-kindergarten through first grade for the last 25 years. She currently teaches kindergarten. She had a delightful time swimming with the dolphins at Marineland in Florida. She and her husband Chris live in Roanoke Rapids, NC. They have 2 grown sons, Paul and Lee. You can visit Ms. Wicker's website at www.pinkflamingolady.com.

Index

(Numbers in bold refer to photographs.)

For information on the world's longest-running study of wild dolphins, or to help support ongoing research projects, go to **Mote Marine Laboratory**'s web site, www.mote.org. Mote Marine Laboratory, Sarasota, Florida.

Marineland, the world's first oceanarium, invites you to join them in creating your own lasting memories at the Dolphin Conservation Center. See www.marineland.net. Marineland, St. Augustine, Florida.

The **Wild Dolphin Project** is engaged in a long-term scientific study of a specific pod of Atlantic spotted dolphins that live 40 miles off the coast of the Bahamas in the Atlantic Ocean. Learn more at www.wilddolphinproject.com.

If you enjoyed reading this book, here are some other Pineapple Press titles you might enjoy as well. To request our complete catalog or to place an order, write to Pineapple Press, P.O. Box 3889, Sarasota, Florida 34230, or call 1-800-PINEAPL (746-3275). Or visit our website at www.pineapplepress.com.

Those Amazing Alligators by Kathy Feeney. Illustrated by Steve Weaver, photographs by David M. Dennis. Alligators are amazing animals, as you'll see in this book. Discover the differences between alligators and crocodiles; learn what alligators eat, how they communicate, and much more. Ages 5–9.

Those Outrageous Owls by Laura Wyatt. Illustrated by Steve Weaver, photographs by H. G. Moore III. Learn what owls eat, how they hunt, and why they look the way they do. You'll find out what an owlet looks like, why horned owls have horns, and much more! Ages 5–9.

Those Terrific Turtles by Sarah Cussen. Illustrated by Steve Weaver, photographs by David M. Dennis. You'll learn the difference between a turtle and a tortoise, and find out why they have shells. Meet baby turtles and some very, very old ones, and even explore a pond. Ages 5–9.

Those Excellent Eagles by Jan Lee Wicker. Illustrated by Steve Weaver, photographs by H.G. Moore III. Learn all about those excellent eagles—what they eat, how fast they fly, why the American Bald Eagle is our nation's national bird. You'll even make some edible eagles! Ages 5–9.

Those Peculiar Pelicans by Sarah Cussen. Illustrated by Steve Weaver, photographs by Roger Hammond. Find out how much food those peculiar pelicans can fit in their beaks, how they stay cool, whether they really steal fish from fishermen. And learn how to fold up an origami pelican. Ages 5–9.

Those Funny Flamingos by Jan Lee Wicker. Illustrated by Steve Weaver. Flamingos are indeed funny birds. Learn why those funny flamingos are pink, stand on one leg, eat upside down, and much more. Ages 5–9.

America's Real First Thanksgiving by Robyn Gioia. When most Americans think of the first Thanksgiving, they think of the Pilgrims and the Indians in New England in 1621, but on September 8, 1565, the Spanish and the native Timucua celebrated with a feast of Thanksgiving in St. Augustine, Florida. Ages 9–14.

Drawing Florida Wildlife by Frank Lohan. The clearest, easiest method yet for learning to draw Florida's birds, reptiles, amphibians, and mammals. All ages.

Dinosaurs of the South by Judy Cutchins and Ginny Johnston. Dinosaurs lived in the southeastern United States. Loaded with full-color fossil photos as well as art to show what the dinos might have looked like. Ages 8–12.

Ice Age Giants of the South by Judy Cutchins and Ginny Johnston. Learn about the huge animals and reptiles that lived here during the Ice Age. Meet saber-toothed cats, dire wolves, mammoths, giant sloths, and more. Ages 8–12.

Giant Predators of the Ancient Seas by Judy Cutchins and Ginny Johnston. Meet the giant creatures that prowled the waters of prehistory. Ages 8–12.

Florida A to Z by Susan Jane Ryan. Illustrated by Carol Tornatore. From Alligator to Zephyrhills—200 facts and pictures on Florida history, geography, nature, and people. Ages 8–12.

Florida Lighthouses for Kids by Elinor De Wire. Learn why some lighthouses are tall and some short, why a cat parachuted off St. Augustine Lighthouse, and much more. Lots of color pictures. Ages 9 and up.